P9-CKF-174

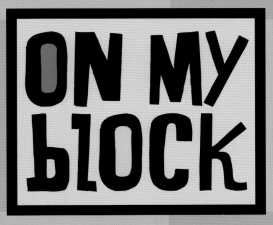

ON MY BLOCK

STORIES AND PAINTINGS
BY FIFTEEN ARTISTS

EDITED BY DANA GOLDBERG

CHILDREN'S BOOK PRESS
SAN FRANCISCO, CALIFORNIA

Cecilia Álvarez

My *abuelita* Conchita's garden in Tijuana was a jungle of flowers, bushes, and fruit trees. *Abuelita* had a green thumb and could grow plants that weren't supposed to grow in that part of Baja California, like papayas. I loved going to my grandmother's house after school because I knew my cousins would be there, ready to play *colores* or hide and seek. We would sit in the fig trees, eating figs and watching all the birds, insects, and butterflies float by. My grandmother's garden was the hub of our social world, where we played, heard wonderful stories, and ate delicious *merienda* food prepared by my aunts.

I grew up on the other side of the border, in California, just five miles from my *abuelita* and five blocks from the ocean. I was so lucky to grow up in a magical place where the desert meets the Pacific Ocean, and where my relations lived in two different countries, yet were so close to each other.

Cecilia Álvarez is a fine artist who lives, paints, and teaches in Seattle, Washington. She was raised between San Diego, California, and Ensenada, Baja California in Mexico. Cecilia is also the illustrator of *Antonio's Card*, a children's book.

Photo by Dana Goldberg

ON MY BLOCK
hawaii Cinerama Theater

CARL ANGEL

When I was a boy, the Hawaii Cinerama Theater in downtown Honolulu was the first place I could go by myself. Or should I say it was the first place I could go to travel the galaxy?

Inside it was dark like outer space, and the seats were like those in a rocket ship. I always sat in the center row surrounded by my crew of fellow space travelers, dressed in our uniforms of tank tops, flip flops, and shorts. The screen would start to flicker and we'd blast off from the island and journey to other worlds like Nebula 6, the Phantom Zone, and Paris.

When the lights came up and I returned to Earth, I would take my sketch pad and my lunch of rice, macaroni salad, and Kalua pig to the beach and draw what I had seen in my travels. But sometimes it wasn't enough, and I would have to make a second trip that day!

Photo by Holly Kim

Carl Angel is a fine artist, graphic designer, and the illustrator of *Lakas and the Makibaka Hotel*. Born in Maryland and raised in Hawaii, Carl now lives and paints in San Leandro, California.

CARL ANGEL 5

Cbabi Bayoc

The coolest thing about our neighborhood, besides the fantastic 100-year-old brick homes and the wonderful diversity of people, is that we live down the block from a beautiful park— or, as my daughter says, the "park-park."

The park is extremely family-friendly: full of gazebos, majestic trees, and a pond that attracts almost every newly married couple for wedding photographs. In the spring and summer, you can watch softball games with players who are five years old to fifty-five years old.

But with all that, nothing equals the excitement of the "park-park." The "park-park" is the playground section where kids ask their parents to push them on swings for hours, dangle from monkey bars with their friends, and gleefully whoosh down the slide over and over again. For my family, the "park-park" is where memories are made.

Cbabi Bayoc is a fine artist and illustrator whose artwork reflects his love of music and family. His work can be found in homes, galleries, and in the book *Young Cornrows Callin Out the Moon.* He lives in St. Louis, Missouri, with his wife and children.

Photo by Reine Bayoc

Kim Cogan

I'm a full-time artist, and I spend most of my time in my studio. I call my studio "The Lab" because it is filled with many jars and bottles, similar to a scientist's laboratory. Like a scientist, I think of new ideas and experiment with how to create my paintings.

Inside, it smells of linseed oil and oil paint. Beside my easel there are tubes of paint, my palette, brushes, and tools. Canvases line the walls, some blank, some in progress, and some finished paintings. Sometimes friends come by to see what is new, but often the new paintings are already off to a dealer who will sell them.

I paint what is around me daily, people and neighborhoods, whatever captures my eye or sparks my interest. When I am inspired I paint intensely, as if there was a burning fire inside of me and the only way to put it out is to get the idea out of my head, through the brush in my hands, and onto the canvas!

Kim Cogan was born in Pusan, Korea, and grew up in the San Francisco Bay Area. An acclaimed painter, he also illustrated *Cooper's Lesson.* He can be found in his art studio or surfing the waves off of San Francisco's Ocean Beach.

Photo by Janet del Mundo

MAYA
Christina
Gonzalez

When I was seven years old, I had an accident. It was serious, and I was unconscious in a coma for three days. When I woke up there were gifts that good friends and family had left for me. That's when I received my first real art materials: a pad of newsprint paper especially for drawing and some colored pencils. These made me feel like I could draw forever. Images popped into my head every time I looked at an empty page. And my hands felt like birds ready to fly, they wanted to draw so much.

Each page felt like an open sky waiting for me. And I would draw and draw and draw. The empty page remains one of my favorite places to fly.

Maya Christina Gonzalez grew up in the Mojave Desert. Her artwork has been featured on the cover of *Chicano/a Art*. Maya has also illustrated nearly a dozen books for children, including *My Very Own Room* and *Nana's Big Surprise*.

Photo by Marilyn Smith

yasmin Hernandez

Storybooks I read as a child always talked about magical forests and castles, farms and their many animals. Whenever one heard about Brooklyn, it seemed to be the tough city, dirty and gray. But I knew different. On the walls of our apartment, my mom painted pictures of our island home, Puerto Rico. Rooftops were my playground, where I pretended to be a superhero with special powers. Every summer there were block parties with salsa music and early hip-hop songs like "Planet Rock" or "Play at Your Own Risk." People would ride by on cool motorcycles wearing leather jackets decorated with the Puerto Rican flag. This was the beautiful and exciting Brooklyn of my childhood.

This painting includes my brother Joseph's graffiti, to celebrate people like him who use art and music to make our neighborhoods come to life. Though others may think that growing up poor or in a "not-so-nice" neighborhood should bring us shame, we find beauty and pride in every-thing. Our experience is just as special, just as beautiful as any other. This is for all the children (big and small) who take risks, live freely, and see the world as it should be!

Brooklyn-born and raised, Yasmin Hernandez is an award-winning painter and installation artist. In addition to creating artwork and lecturing, she is also an artist-educator at El Museo del Barrio and the Studio Museum in Harlem, in New York City.

Photo by John James

14 FELICIA HOSHINO

Felicia Hoshino

Miso, aburage, konnyaku, natto, and *tofu*… These Japanese foods were foreign to me growing up on macaroni and cheese. My dad Ed, on the other hand, woke up to the smells of these foods cooking in the kitchen… and the basement! From their home in San Francisco's Japantown, my dad's family operated Norio Company from the time they were released from the Poston Internment Camp in 1945, until redevelopment forced them out of the neighborhood in the early 1970's.

My grandparents, Minoru and Chizuko Arikawa, and eventually my dad and his brother Thom, labored through the long process of fermenting soybeans into  their main product, *miso* paste. They also spent the early hours of each morning soaking, grinding, and boiling soybeans and then straining, curdling, and molding soymilk into the freshest *tofu* to be delivered to local Japanese restaurants.

Today when I go to Japantown to buy *miso, aburage, konnyaku, natto,* and *tofu*, I often think about my grandparents' house and wonder what it would have been like, waking up each morning to the warm sweet smell of soybeans cooking in the kitchen… and the basement!

Felicia Hoshino was born in San Francisco, California, where she lives today with her husband and son. She is a mixed-media artist and illustrator whose award-winning work can be seen in magazines and children's books such as *A Place Where Sunflowers Grow.*

Photo by Yoshi Hoshino

Sara Kahn

Shaggy, Grumpy and Stripey were three of the thirty-two cats I played with in my grandparents' garden in Tehran when I was a little girl. My grandma did not want to keep pets in the house, but she loved feeding the stray cats that visited the garden. The cats basked in the sun, climbed the old pear tree, drank water from the little pond, snacked on the food my grandma put out, and chased each other around.

I named every one of the thirty-two cats, played hide and seek with them, and when we got tired we all had a catnap on the bench.

Sara Kahn has loved painting—and cats— since she was a little girl. She now lives in San Francisco with her husband and three cats, including Zemmy (pictured). Her award-winning illustrations can be seen in children's magazines and anthologies.

Photo by Steve Kahn

Conan Low

When I was growing up, every Saturday evening my *tai-pau* (great-grandmother) would gather her children, grandchildren, and great-grand-children into her tiny one-bedroom flat in San Francisco. It was so crowded it was almost impossible to get past the giant pile of shoes at the front door.

Holidays were extra special. On Thanksgiving we would line up in the kitchen for my favorite meal of turkey and gravy on sticky rice. At Christmas it was a contest to see whose new boyfriend would be stuffed into our old plastic Santa suit. Most of the time, though, the role of Santa was relegated to my Uncle Steve.

These days our family is too big to get together every week, but we still gather on holidays. My wife and I now pass out *lai see*—lucky red envelopes —at our house on Chinese New Year, and someday soon I'm sure there will be a mountain of shoes at our front door.

Conan Low is a proud cancer survivor and artist. He has worked on various animated films and tv shows, although he still prefers his favorite media: pencil, paint, and Legos. He lives, plays, and gardens with his wife in Northern California.

Photo by Lori Low

Joseph Pearson

Storytelling has a long history in the African American community, dating back to ancient Africa.

This image suggests a time from my childhood when we kids would gather around the feet of the "ol' heads," as my dad called adults, and listen to their tales. Some were funny and filled with riddles, while others were very scary and caused many sleepless nights. The porch was the usual gathering place for these happy times.

I continued that tradition with my daughter. I began reading to her at an early age. When she was but a baby I told her stories relevant to our history. The balloons are an element from my life's experiences. They are intended to suggest hope and the reality that life is fleeting and fragile.

Joseph Pearson was born in Pearl River County, on the Mississippi Gulf Coast. He has been a full-time artist for nearly three decades. He lives with his wife in Alexandria, Louisiana, where they relocated after Hurricane Katrina.

Photo by Olan Mills

Elaine Pedlar

My favorite place to be when I was growing up was the bottom bunk in the room I shared with my three sisters. We lived in a cramped apartment with my three brothers and my mom and dad in the Hammels projects of Rockaway Beach, Queens, New York.

In our apartment, there was rarely a quiet moment to be alone. But in the bottom bunk, tucked in with my imagination, I would pull the covers over my head and disappear. I drew on anything I could get my hands on—on brown paper grocery bags, or in a sketchbook I might have gotten for a special occasion like a birthday or Christmas. One of my favorite things to sketch on was the cardboard that came inside my mom's pantyhose packages.

I mostly drew dancing ladies in colored dresses with shining faces, elaborate hairstyles, and the latest jewelry. I would sign the pages and tuck them underneath the mattress until it bulged. I loved it there. I felt safe there. It was my little world.

Elaine Pedlar was born in Queens, New York, the youngest girl of seven children. Since graduating from Parsons School of Design in 1987, she has been a fashion designer. She is also the illustrator of the book *A Shelter In Our Car.* Elaine lives in Brooklyn, New York.

Photo by Brian Sullivan

ON MY bLOCK
the PACIFIC Shoreline

Ann Phong was born in Vietnam. After escaping by boat in 1981, she settled in Southern California. Ann is an internationally exhibited painter and the illustrator of *Going Home, Coming Home*. She teaches art at California State Polytechnic University, Pomona.

ANN PHONG

The ocean always attracts me. I often go to Long Beach, in Southern California, to dip my feet in the soft sand. The people strolling along the seashore, children flying kites, and the young guys surfing all remind me of my home country, Vietnam, on the other side of the Pacific Ocean.

Over there, fish merchants go to the seashore early every morning. They buy the freshest fish from the fishermen who have just come back from the previous night's catch. Fish are everywhere and people are everywhere, too. The ocean is my favorite spot, and scenes from both shores of the Pacific always stay in my mind every time I hear the water splash.

José Ramírez

I remember playing baseball out on my block, on Ithaca Avenue in East Los Angeles. Every day after we finished our homework we'd run outside, bat in hand. Eddie, Fernie, Jorge, Willy, Javier, Beto, Omar (my brother), and I would split into teams — the Yankees against the Dodgers. We'd dodge around parked cars and neighbors while trying to score runs or catch fly balls. Other kids would just hang out, ride their bikes, or cheer for their friends.

It was fun playing, except when someone got hurt or we lost the ball in the bushes. One time we broke the windshield of my dad's truck—we were grounded for a few weeks after that one. Most of the time we played until it got dark. Then we'd go inside, shower, watch tv, and get ready for the next day of school — and baseball.

Photo by Lariza Dugan-Cuadra

José Ramírez was born in Los Angeles, California, where he still lives today. An artist, muralist, and the illustrator of *Quinito's Neighborhood,* José also teaches second grade in the Los Angeles Unified School District.

JOSÉ RAMÍREZ 27

Tonel

When I was nine or ten years old my family moved from Marianao to another part of Havana called La Lisa. One of our new neighbors was Joseíto, who was from the countryside. He decided one day to build a fence around the empty lot next door, and to use the land as if it were a small farm located right in the heart of the city. Everybody began calling that piece of land "Joseíto's little farm."

Joseíto grew bananas, beans, tomatoes, corn, and avocados, depending on the season. He also had a few chickens and a very colorful rooster running around, as well as some ducks, a goat, and a pig. Sometimes big frogs jumped in the grass, especially after a good summer rainfall. When it was time to harvest, Joseíto always came upstairs to bring us a few ripe bananas, a large green avocado, or a paper bag filled with freshly picked black beans.

Photo by Adolfo Lopez Otero

Tonel was born in Havana, Cuba. His work has been exhibited in Cuba since 1973, and internationally since the early 1980's. Tonel is the illustrator of *Drum, Chavi, Drum!* and an Adjunct Professor at the University of British Columbia, Vancouver, Canada.

JONATHAN WARMDAY

On a winter night sprinkled with countless stars, smoke from burning *piñon* wood comes through the chimneys. My younger brother and I walk ahead of our parents, guided by the glowing moon rising over the mountains. We're on our way to our grandparents' winter home within the old walls of Taos Pueblo.

We are greeted by the sight, sound, and smell of cedar wood crackling in the *horno* with the promise of delicious bread and cookies. Later, wide-eyed, we will sit in front of the warm, inviting fireplace, listening to old tribal stories of coyote the trickster.

I can still remember . . .

Jonathan Warmday is a renowned painter who grew up on the Taos Pueblo Indian Reservation. He resides there today with his two daughters, who attend a nearby university. He is also the illustrator of *Kiki's Journey,* a children's book.

Photo by Giovanna Paponetti

ON MY BLOCK

A decade after Children's Book Press published its first two artists' anthologies, it struck me that a natural theme for another such book would be the idea of place. We asked fifteen talented fine artists, some of whom we knew well and some new faces, to ponder the places that mean the most to them. They offered places here and abroad, from their childhoods or from their current neighborhoods, places that have influenced their creative lives as artists, and places they know through stories they've heard from family members. The spots these artists chose might not be marked with fancy plaques or statues, but nevertheless represent an important part of who they are. Take a look around you. Who are you, and where have you been?

—Dana Goldberg, Editor

Overall book project copyright © 2007 by Children's Book Press. All rights reserved. Each individual artist's entry is copyrighted in the artist's name:
Page 2-3 © 2007 by Cecilia Álvarez; page 4-5 © 2007 by Carl Angel; page 6-7 © 2007 by Cbabi Bayoc; page 8-9 © 2007 by Kim Cogan; page 10-11 © 2007 by Maya Christina Gonzalez; page 12-13 © 2007 by Yasmin Hernandez; page 14-15 © 2007 by Felicia Hoshino; page 16-17 © 2007 by Sara Kahn; page 18-19 © 2007 by Conan Low; page 20-21 © 2007 by Joseph Pearson; page 22-23 © 2007 by Elaine Pedlar; page 24-25 © 2007 by Ann Phong; page 26-27 © 2007 by José Ramírez; page 28-29 © 2007 by Tonel; page 30-31 © 2007 by Jonathan Warmday.

Editor: Dana Goldberg
Design & Production: Lorena Piñon, Pinwheel Design
Production Coordinator: Janine Macbeth
Thanks to: Harriet Rohmer for her two previous inspired anthologies; Rachel Sher for her indispensable help with fundraising; Dr. Stephen Mallory and his daughter for being Joseph Pearson's models; and the staff of CBP: Imelda, Janet, Lori, Lorraine, Patricia, and Rod.

The organizations listed below are committed to creative expression, education, and preserving the cultural heritage and wellbeing of children and their communities. They recognized our shared interest in community involvement and child welfare, and contributed to the creation of this book. Children's Book Press offers its gratitude to all of them:

American Federation of Teachers:
www.aft.org

Association of Hispanic Arts, Inc.:
www.latinoarts.org

Children's Fairyland:
www.fairyland.org

Chinese Culture Center:
www.c-c-c.org

Citizen's Committee for Children of New York, Inc.: www.cccnewyork.org

Coleman Advocates for Children and Youth:
www.colemanadvocates.org

Destiny Arts Center:
www.destinyarts.org

Greenlining Institute:
www.greenlining.org

Japanese Cultural and Community Center of Northern California:
www.jcccnc.org

Manilatown Heritage Foundation:
www.manilatown.org

Oakland Asian Students Educational Services:
www.oases.org

Oakland Ready to Learn:
www.oaklandreadytolearn.org

St. Michael's Guatemala Project:
www.cprguatemalaproject.org

Printed in Hong Kong via Marwin Productions
10 9 8 7 6 5 4 3 2 1

Library of Congress
Cataloging in Publication Data:

On my block : stories and paintings by fifteen artists / edited by Dana Goldberg.
     p. cm.
ISBN-13: 978-0-89239-220-9 (hardcover)
ISBN-10: 0-89239-220-7 (hardcover)
1. Minority artists—United States—Psychology—Juvenile literature. 2. Place (Philosophy)—Juvenile literature. I. Goldberg, Dana, 1975-
N6537.5.O5 2007
704'.089—dc22
                              2007000393

Children's Book Press is a nonprofit publisher of multicultural literature for children. For a catalog, write: Children's Book Press, 2211 Mission Street, San Francisco, CA 94110. Visit our website: www.childrensbookpress.org

For sales information, please contact Children's Book Press. Quantity discounts are available through the publisher for educational or nonprofit use.